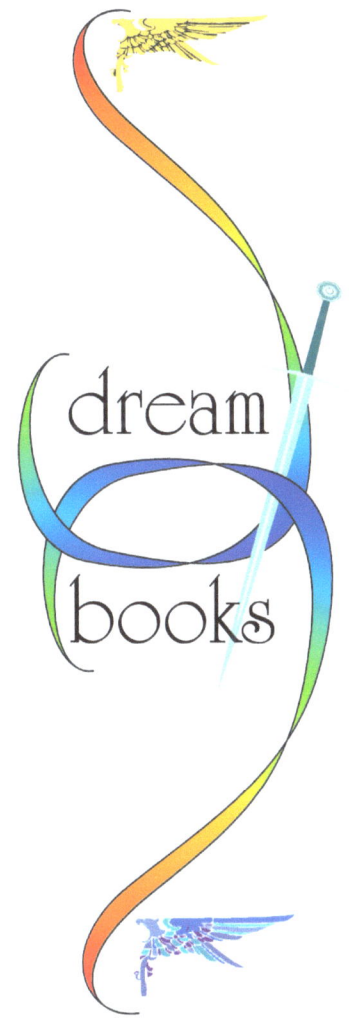

Prophetic Interpretation of Art
© Copyright Sheri Hauser 2020
© Copyright Karna Peck 2008
Published by Glorybound Publishing, Camp Verde, AZ. USA
SAN 256-4564
10 9 8 7 6 5 4 3 2 1
2nd Edition
Printed in the United States of America
Art from the gallery of Karna Peck
KDP ISBN 9781081521165
Copyright data is available on file.
Hauser, Sheri, 1957-
        Prophetic Interpretation of Art/Sheri Hauser
        Includes biographical reference.
1. Religious/Prophecy.   2. Spiritual Art.   I. Title

www.gloryboundpublishing.com
www.karnapeck.com

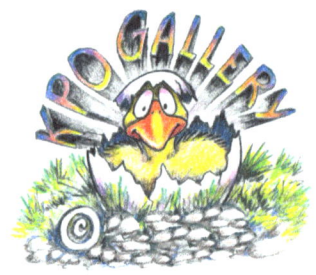

All of the art included in this book was taken from the gallery of Karna Peck. You can order her art www.karnapeckcom

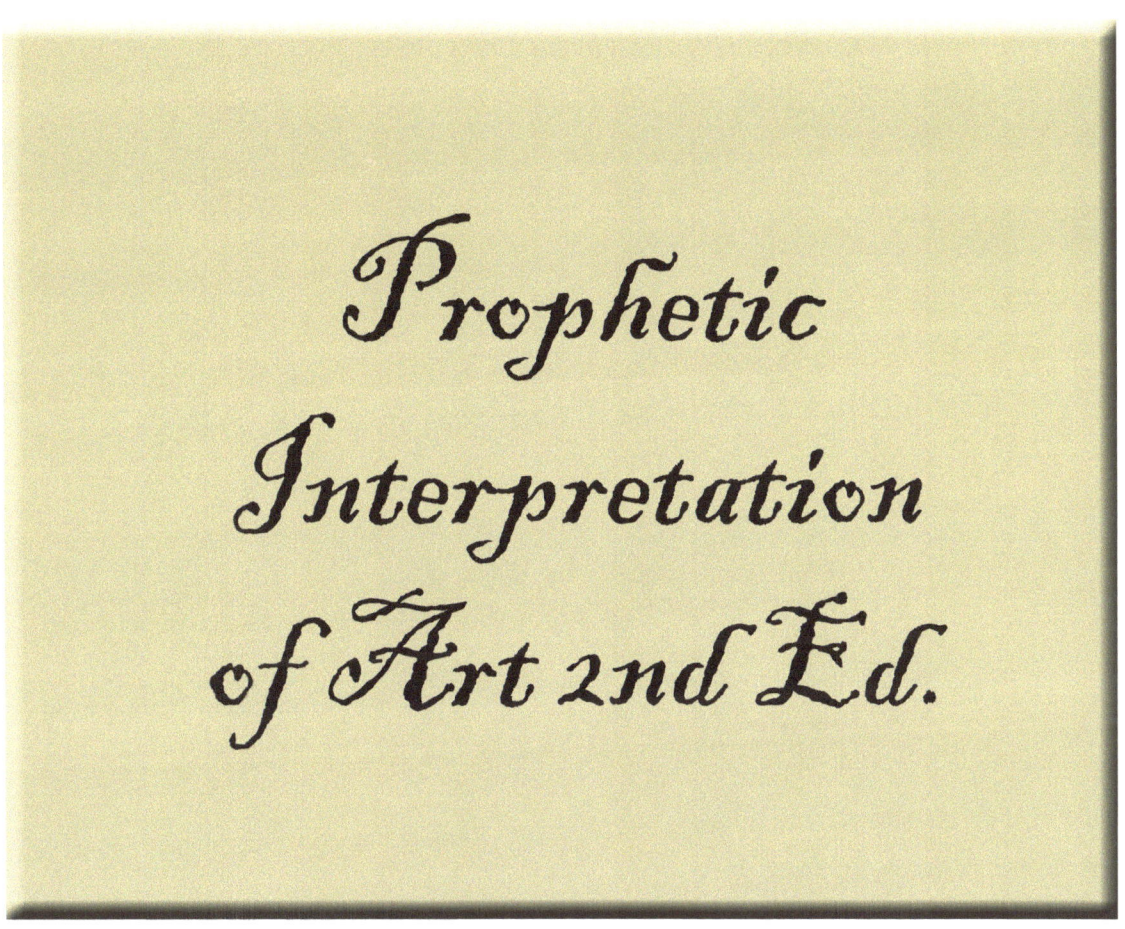

Prophetic Interpretation of Art 2nd Ed.

Art by Karna Peck
Interpretation by Sheri Hauser

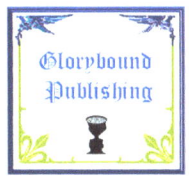

Glorybound Publishing
Camp Verde, Arizona, USA
in the year 2020

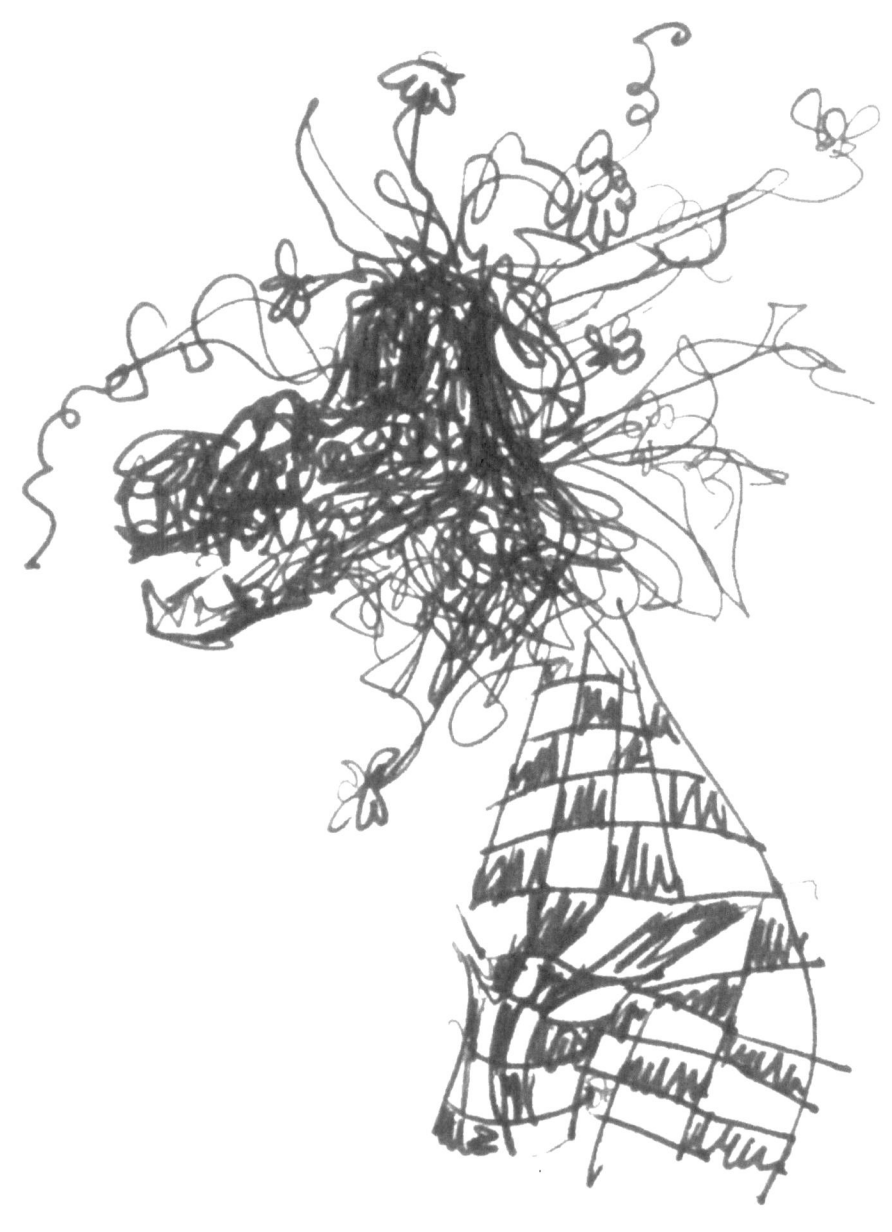

Scribble Monster

Letter from the Author

I am happy to release this book on Prophetic Art which uses art from my sister's gallery. I write books on dreams and interpretation of dreams. When I went to Karna's house and studied the art on her walls, I began to realize that art which hangs on the walls is similar to dreams in that they are pictures with hidden messages.

There are many levels of interpretation and it is important to point out that the message which Karna received when she did the paintings is different from the one which she sought to convey. And, the message which the one who sees the art gets is, still a different message. In essence, there are many messages for the same piece of art.

With the way that I interpret dreams {and art} is that, in order to consider the message to be a spiritual message it must correlate with Scriptures. That is the only 'box' that I draw around the interpretation.
This book is written as a 'challenge' for art lovers to seek the deeper messages which are embedded in the piece and try to see if there is a message from God.
Have Fun.   Sheri

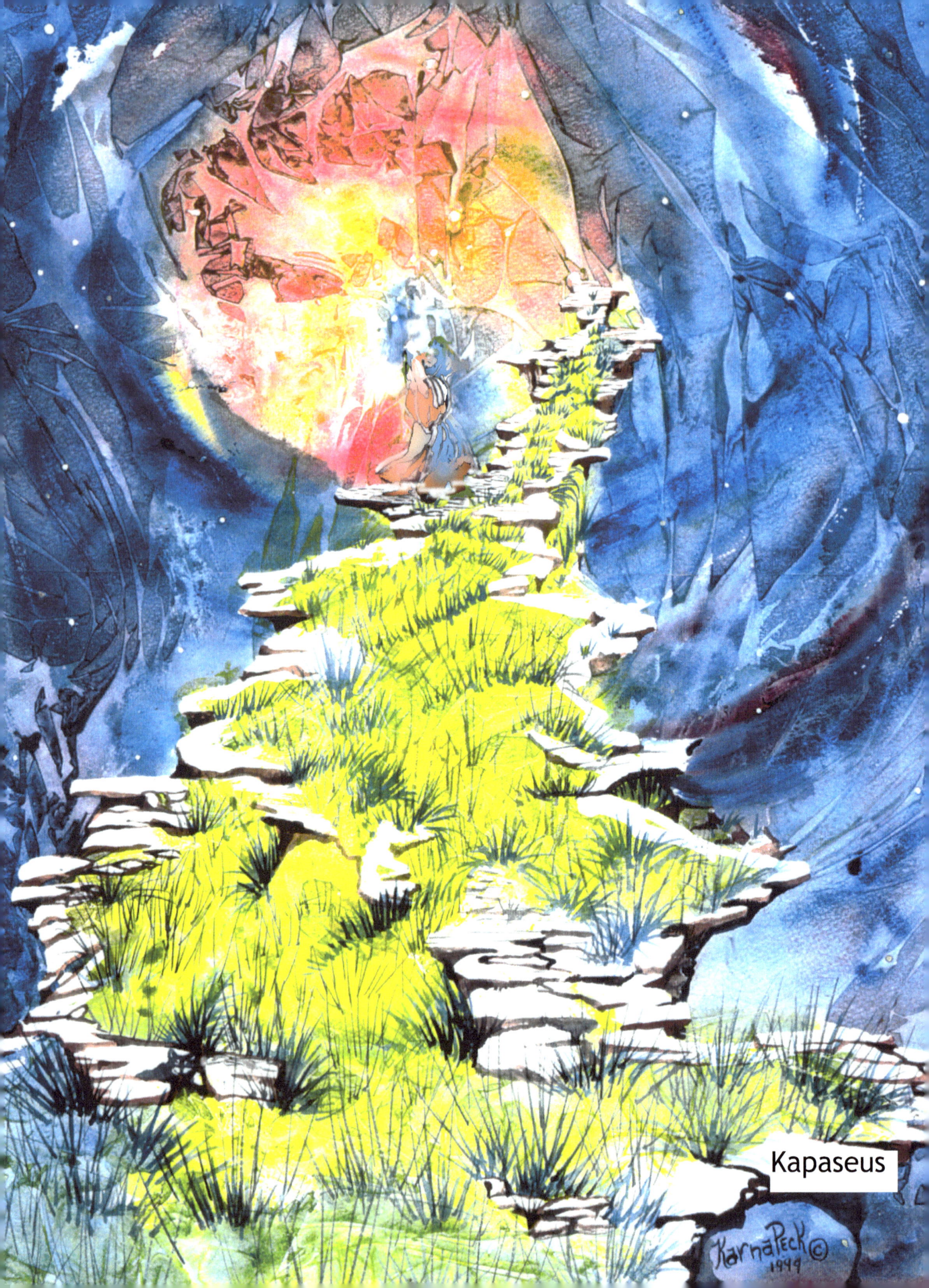

Kapaseus

Prophetic Art

Definition of Art

Art is the activity of using the imagination and skill to create beautiful things. Works such as painting result from this creativity. It is a non scientific branch of learning.

Def. (when a person is stressed, he sings.) An artesian well is drilled deep enough to reach water that rises by internal pressure without pumping. The Holy Spirit becomes in us a well rising up...

My Vision

There is a geyser. It is aqua blue and bubbly. I have the underwater camera view. There are trees along the banks with their roots extended into the water. They are different kinds; spruce, redwood, and pine. All tall and beautiful, green and stately. There are many small trails leading through the trees to the water. The Water has what looks like chemical deposits along the bank. Looks like calcium deposits because there is a discoloration along the shore.

The Word of The Lord came to me, "The water is alive and happy to have found a place to release the pressure."

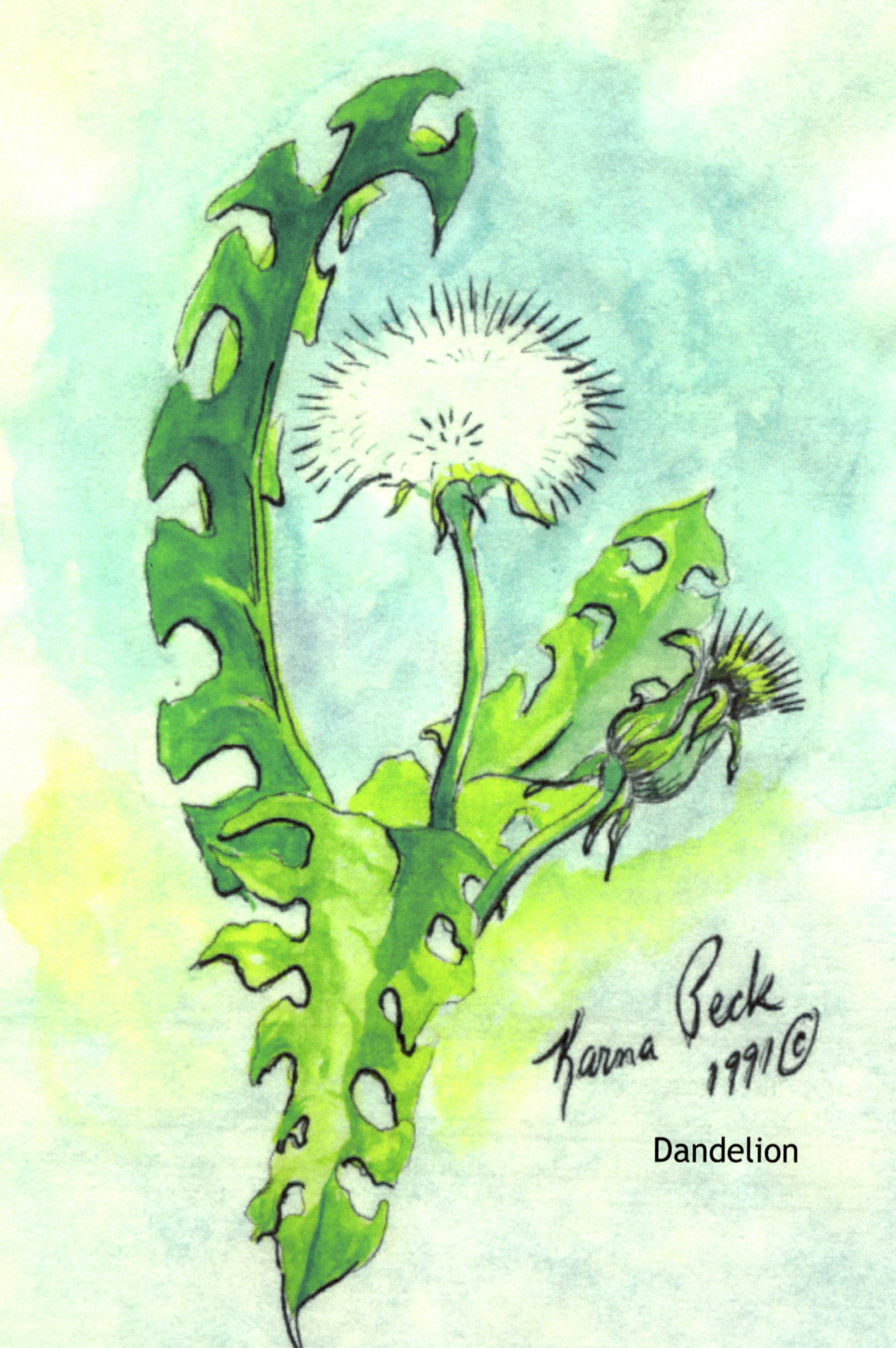

Karna Beck
1991 ©

Dandelion

Interpretation

The geyser is the power of God displayed in the water. The Water is the presence of God coming to us as we yearn for him. He comes to us. The water is what comes to us as we thirst after God initially. It satisfies our soul, fills us and flows through us.

The Spirit of God is recorded as moving on the face of the waters before the earth was created. Jesus Christ was there with him because the world was created through him. He comes to cleanse us of all sin and allow us to sit in a place of perfect Holiness in communion with God. He provides running water, like rivers, to cleanse away every impurity out of our lives. Just as the chemicals are along the bank of the water; Jesus has invested himself in the 'bank' of meeting the Justification needs of the Father for sin. Our sins are deposited in his 'bank' along the edge of the water when we come to God and receive cleansing. He takes our sins on himself just as the water takes on the chemicals from the surrounding rocks. God is called 'The Rock' and we are likened to little rocks, little gems.

There are trails leading down to the water. They are narrow and look like single file hiking. Each person must come to Christ down their own trail. We come to him and learn to drink from him. When we get to the water, we first wash, then we deposit our impurities in his Water. It looks like chemicals around a pool of water.

The large trees are Christians who have their roots in the Water. They are planted in the Kingdom of God in the solid, nutrias soil of the Word of God with their roots

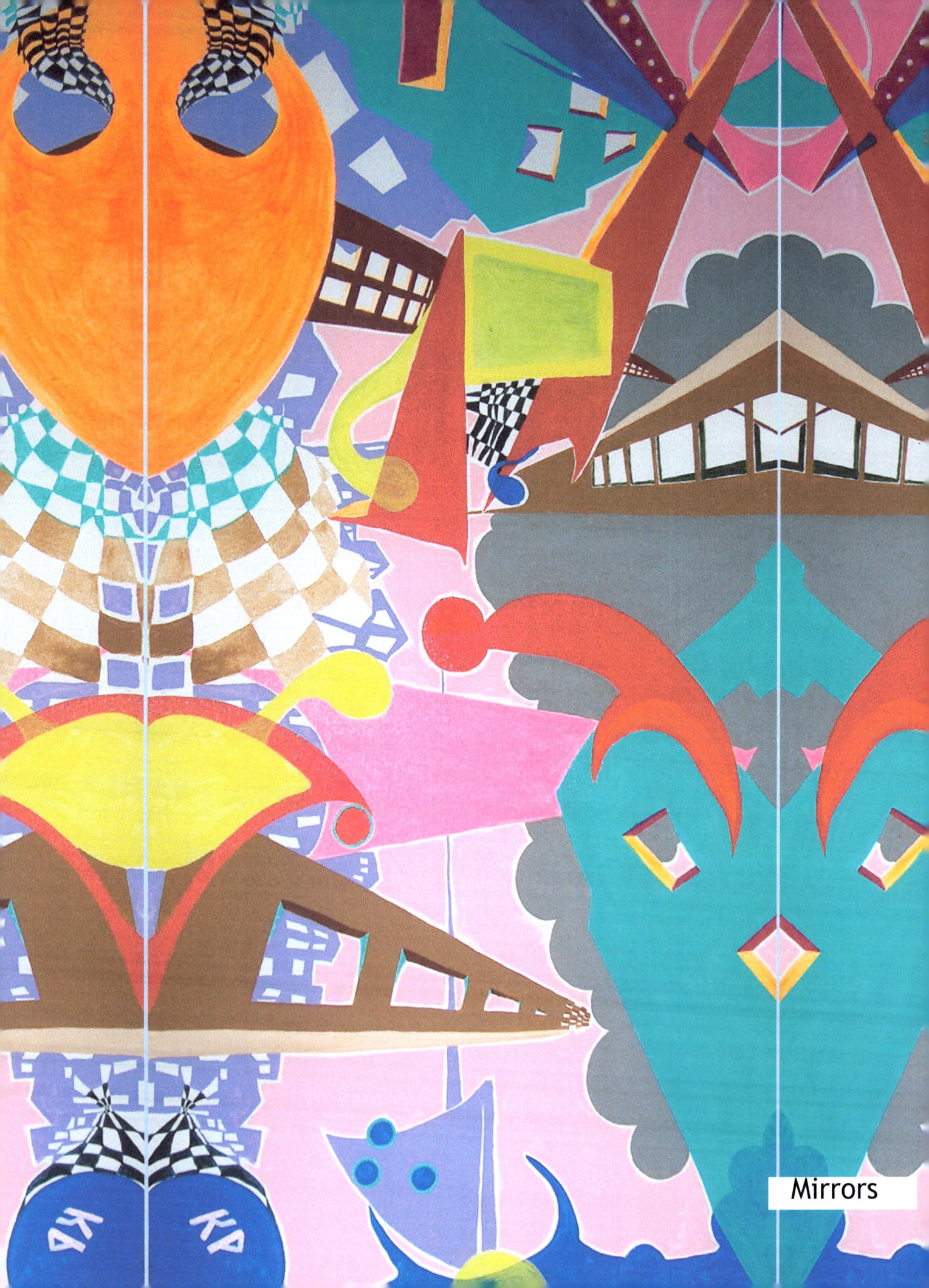

Mirrors

in the water, the Holy Spirit. They provide protection for the new believers that are using the trails to come to Christ, the Living Water.

As the presence of God comes to us, his counsel into our heart brings truths like water drawn from a deep well that we can draw from day after day. His Holy Spirit rises up in us due to internal pressure of the environment he provides to us.

Scripture

This is what the Lord says; "In the time of my favor, I will answer you, and in the day of salvation I will help you; I will keep you and make you to be a covenant for the people, to restore the land and to reassign it's desolate inheritances, to say to the captives 'be free'. They will feed beside the roads and find pasture on every barren hill. The will neither hunger nor thirst, nor will the desert heat or the sun beat upon them. He who has compassion on them will guide them and lead them beside springs of water, and my highways will be raised up. See, they will come from afar -- some from the north, some from the west, some from the region of Aswan. Isaiah 49:8-12

The poor and needy search for water and there is none; their tongues are parched with thirst. But I the Lord will answer them; I the God of Israel, will not forsake them; I will make rivers flow on barren heights, and springs within the valleys. I will turn the desert into pools of water, and the parched ground into springs. I will put the in the desert the cedar and the acacia, the myrtle

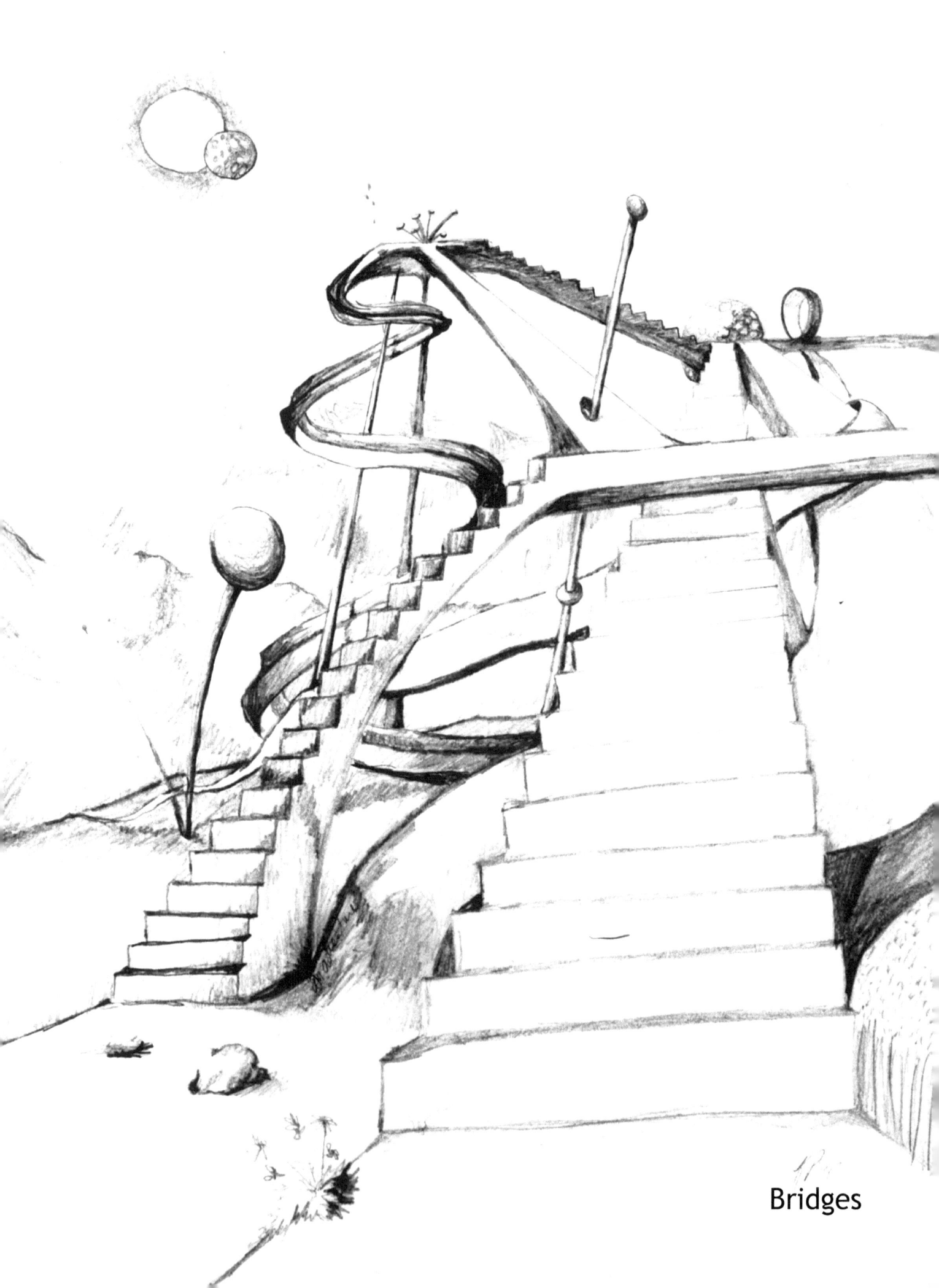

Bridges

and the olive. I will set pines in the wasteland, the fir and the cypress together, so that the people may see and know, may consider and understand, that the hand of the Lord has done this, that the Holy One of Israel has created it. Isaiah 41:17-20

What is Prophetic Art?

God is displayed in all creation

When we pray, God answers us. When He does, often, we don't recognize it because it isn't in a form that we are looking for. We don't see the art as messages from God because we don't fathom His Love for us His constant desire to be in our life. He comes into our world in unusual ways. We were created by God in the beginning to keep Him company. (Gen 3:8). In the beginning Adam and Eve walked side by side with God.   God desires communication with us. He has sought us from the time He created us. We turn away from him. We lost our relationship with Him when Adam and Eve sinned in the Garden of Eden (Gen 3:34).   Every since then He has been working on a plan to get us back into His presence.

He speaks, but often we do not recognize him because we don't recognize his voice. (John 10:4)   And if we don't recognize his voice, how will we know which way to go? Following the voice of God will provide direction

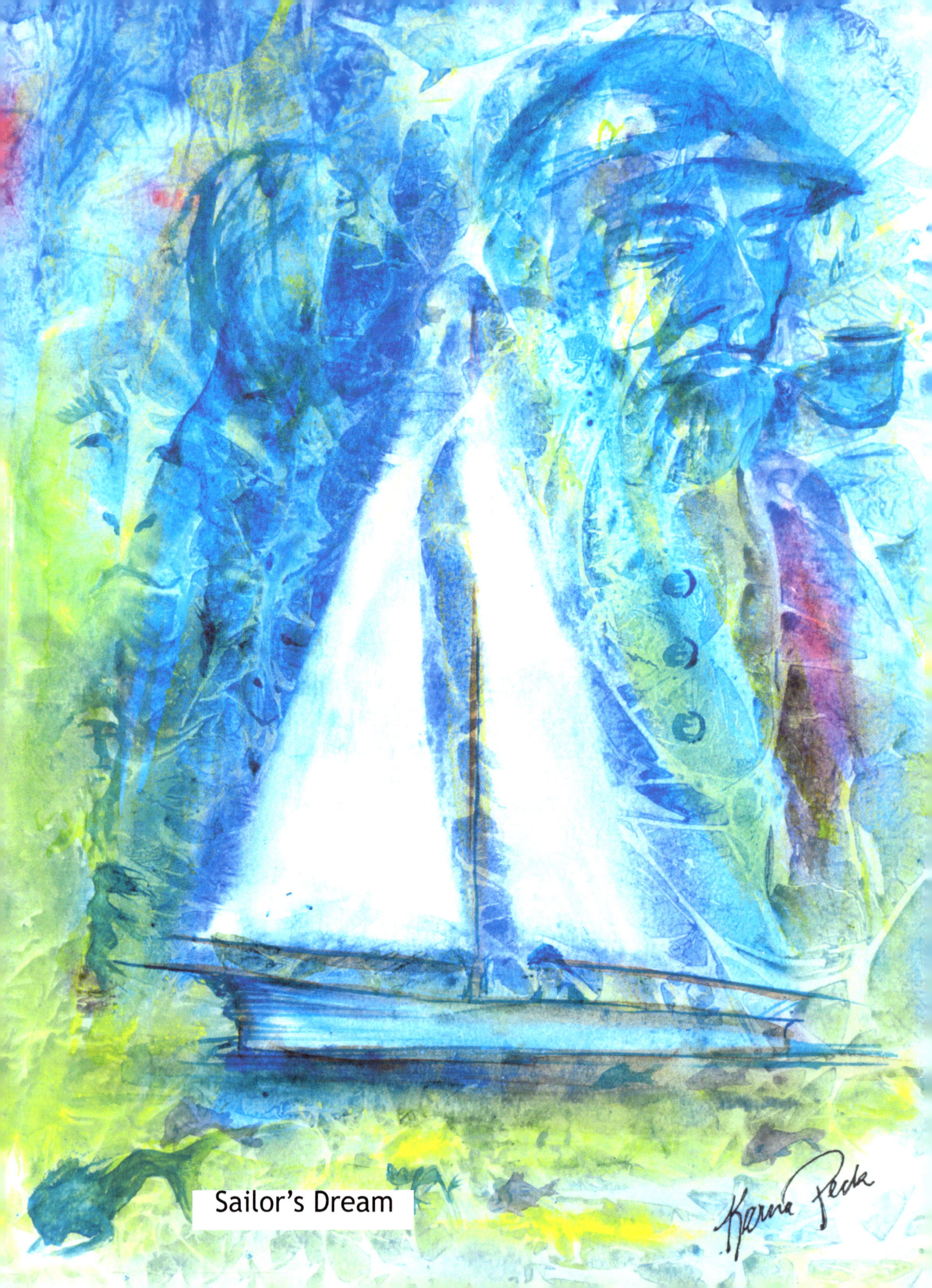

Sailor's Dream

to our lives.

This is how I see God trying to talk to us: He is big, after all he created the whole world including all the galaxies. Let's suppose he wants to get a message to us. Pretend you are big and have a family of ants that you want to get a message to. They would not understand the things in your 'big' world because they only see things from their perspective in the grass.

They don't speak English and you do not speak 'ant language' so the only means of communication you could use is to select things from their environment as teaching tools and demonstrate what you want to teach them. In a similar manner, God doesn't speak 'English' because he is God and we are not. He is so far above us that we can not understand him either. But because he desires to get his messages across, he picks things that we can relate to in our little scope of the world and demonstrates teaching principles.   He gives us visions and we must bring them into our consciousness and transfer them onto a medium that can be visualized with our eyes before we can understand what he wants to teach us.

He uses the things in creation and puts them onto the canvas of our minds. The gifts he has instilled in us transfer them to the canvas. He uses the canvas of our minds to draw his pictures. A picture has to be visualized by an artist before it can be painted. When an artist has this 'vision' burned on his mind, he cannot rest until it is let out by what ever medium he uses to display his ideas. God delivers his messages through assigning individuals to specific duties in the Kingdom of God.

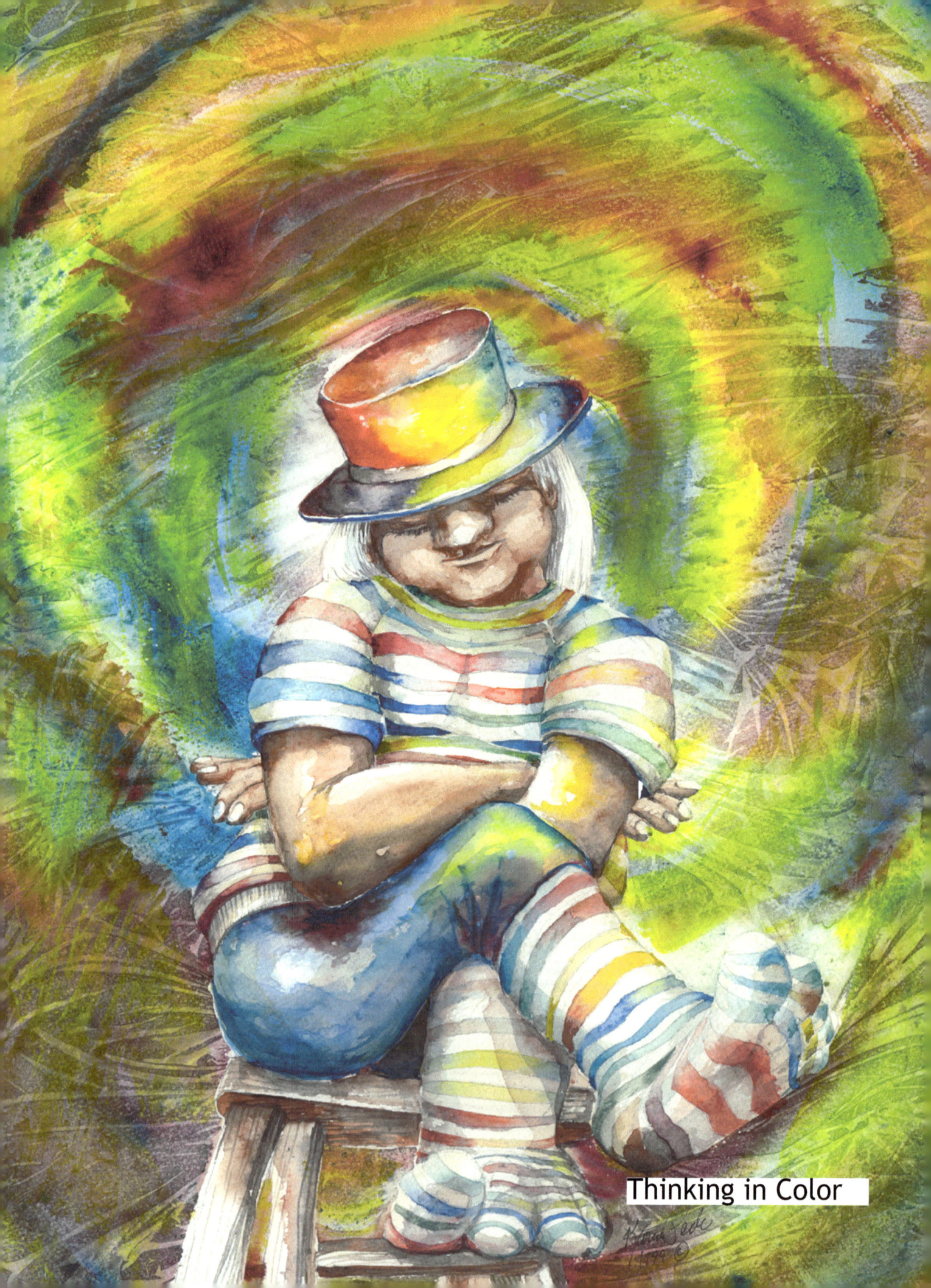

Thinking in Color

Why does He give us the Message?

Our primary purpose is to utilize our talents to praise Him. We have been entrusted with gifts which we are supposed to develop for the use of the Church body. When we become complacent in the use of them, there is a curse of God that will bring withered hands and blindness. Obedience to use the gifts God has entrusted us with allows us to become slaves to righteousness which leads to Holiness. Sharing our gifts with others brings unification of the body of Christ and permits others to enter into our acceptable sacrifice of Praise.

Many times others do not see our 'talent'. We may become discouraged. But , we must remember that we are living in a time that the enemy is fighting hard against us. He knows that he has only a short time and he will be chained in Hell forever. Even though, as loyal servants of Christ, we are spread out, do not be discouraged. He has called us and He will multiply us because of His righteousness. We are supposed to bring everything into the house of God, so the temple can be built. God needs every tool for the Kingdom of God to be built. Just because others may say that your art is bad, in God's eyes it is an essential tool that he needs to display his character and teaching. We are the display of God's righteousness to the world through our gifts in

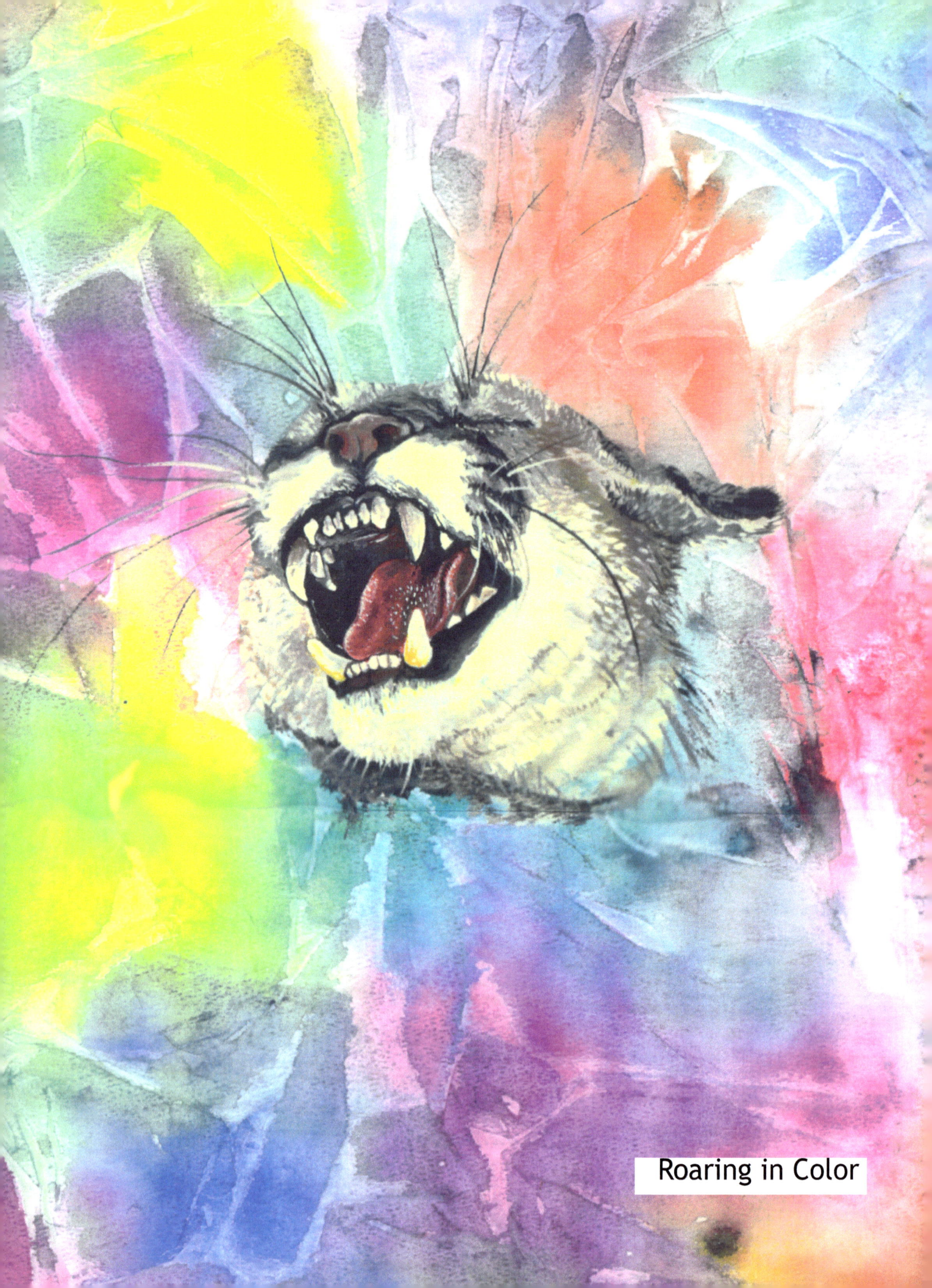

Roaring in Color

unity with our relationship in Christ Jesus. As children of God, he calls us stars in his Kingdom. He wants us to shine for Him.   Just like comets, we are in motion and each display a tail of a different color. No two stars are alike. We all shine for him, but display different characteristics within his Kingdom. There may be many with similar gifts, but each has a wonderful tail of a different color.

Visions and Dreams

A vision is a "Mental representation of external objects, or scenes. An object that comes up in the mind." (Funk & Wagnall's Dictionary).

In order for an artist to paint a picture, he must first have a mental representation of it . It has to be built in his mind. He has to visualize it, dream it. Then, in obedience to the vision, he puts it into action and builds it, "just like he saw it". In essence, artists have visions that are transferred to canvas. The impressions are first 'etched' on their mind, then transferred to the paper for others to see. They try to make it 'just like they saw it.'

There are over one hundred references to dreams and visions in the Bible. Many individuals had visions. In Acts 10, Cornelius has a vision in which God tells him to accept Paul and pray over him to receive his sight again. Each of the book of Prophecy in the Scriptures are visions that have been transferred to paper by the

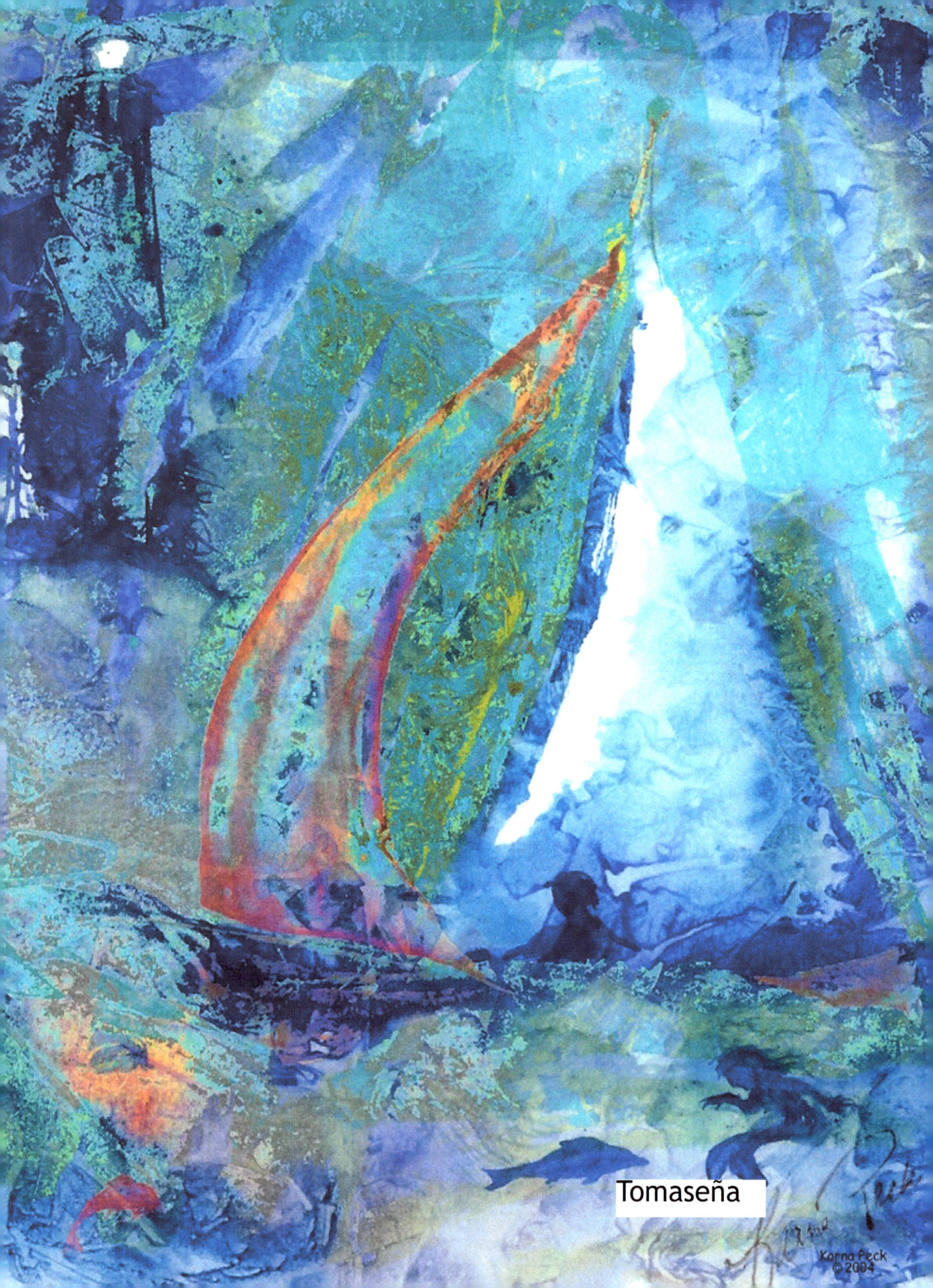

Tomaseña

author when God 'etched' it on their mind. Jeremiah, Ezekiel, and Revelation all are written in symbolic form. They could be 'painted'. They are all visionary and prophetic. Often God speaks to us in an unconventional manner. We need to be open to listen to Him.. We do not limit God when we don't listen to Him, we limit His work in our lives.

Scripture

He who has a dream let him tell it, He who has my word speak it faithfully. What does straw have to do with wheat? Is not my word a fire and a hammer that breaks the rock into pieces? (Jer 23:28-30).

We are not to ignore the visions, but to become faithful to speak their meaning faithfully according to God's intention of the message. The visions are to have a firm foundation in the Scriptures. I do not believe a vision that I cannot find a foundation for. As we trust God for the foundation of each vision, He is faithful. Visions come to life can add tremendous faith to your walk with God.

Artists are Prophets

All artists are prophets, but there are different gifting within the levels of prophecy in the Kingdom of God. Every Christian who has the Holy Spirit dwelling within him, has the 'word of God' etched on their heart. If that individual is an artist, then the Holy Spirit will flow out with greater intensity through their gift of art. Because God encompasses all and all, his voice can even be heard through artists that are not filled with the Holy Spirit and have entered the Kingdom of God through salvation through Jesus Christ.

There are those with a special gift of prophecy who have a close relationship with God. He has taught them to listen well, and tell the desires of his heart to others. They know his character because they have spent time getting to know him. They know that God signs His art work. The deeper level of prophecy is associated with intimacy with Jesus Christ through the Holy Spirit. Paul, in the New Testament, said it was a desire of his heart that all would become prophets to this level. God desires us all to recognize His signature. He is doing a lot of art work that we are not crediting Him for.

Historically, God has spoken to his people through Prophets. A prophet was an individual who became the 'mouthpiece' of God. The Lord would put words into their mouth and send them to speak to groups of people to get them to follow His ways. These individuals were consecrated (set apart) and anointed (given special ability) to do whatever mission God wanted them to do.

Moses, Aaron, Jeremiah, Isaiah, John the Baptist were prophets.

Visions and dreams throughout the Bible provide direction: Daniel 2:3 Nebuchadnezzar had a dream. His spirit became " anxious to understand the dream." He knew that he must interpret the dream because it was telling him how to run the kingdom. The dream ended up being interpreted by Daniel. It provided information needed to warn about a famine that was to come onto the land.

Art is the Word of God visualized: It is special

The Holy Scriptures are different from other words. This is the Word of God. It pierces between our soul and spirit. It is able to judge the thoughts and intentions of the heart (Heb 4:12). Our soul is the self drive of appetites and desires. We know what we want and attempt to get it. The Spirit of man is the activating force within living being. Notice in Genesis that God Breaths into Adam the breath of life. This is the spiritual aspect of Adam being born. (Gen 2:7) .

Art moves both our soul and our spirit. When the art is not understood in relation to God, the creator, then our soul is stirred yet our Spirit remains hungry for God. It is the Breath of the Almighty gives us understanding (Job 32:8).

The Holy Spirit was given to us when Jesus ascended to heaven. He provides us with the ability to know God. He is correlated with 'wind' or breath. We know that no man has the ability to breath apart from God giving him that breath. God retains power over our death and life. This is the essence of the Spirit. It's about the breath: wind provides movement to the walk (Jn 3:8). The spirit of us is the life center retained by God. No man has authority to restrain the wind with the wind, or authority over the day of death: (Ecc 8:8).   When God take away our spirit, we expire (Ps 104:29).

When we become the Breath of God

Many times we think that it is our soul, our will that dominates our moral character. But this is not true. When we are born again, the Holy Spirit takes up residence in our spirit. This Holy Spirit writes his laws on our hearts. He etches his character on us. His character of Holiness. (Prov 16:18, Hos 4:12). His Spirit within us will provide the source of one's insight . It is the Holy Spirit within us that etches the impressions on the mind and then helps us to interpret them to bring them to the paper. (ICor 2:11)

When we become children of God through belief in Jesus Christ as our Savior, we become sensitive to inner voice of Holy Spirit. We receive a spirit of adoption as sons by which we cry out "Abba! Father!.(Rom 8:15). This new adoption enables us to think spiritually dominated by God. The Spirit Himself (God's Holy Spirit) testifies with our spirit that we are children of God (Rom 8:16). The same new spirit gives mind of Christ to believer (I Cor

2:16). You are renewed in the spirit of your mind when you have the new spirit.   When we focus on God, then he will to talk into your mind. He will etch the 'word of God' on your painting. Hebrews 10:16 says, " This is the covenant that I will make with them: After those days, says the Lord: I will put My laws upon their heart, and on their mind I will write them."

When we become Christians, then we are to serve in the midst of the others. We come as an empty vessel, a cup, and he fills us up with whatever he sees will bring us the ultimate happiness.   We hold in our hands whatever we are supposed to give to others on behalf of him. We display his love to the world through the use of our gifts when we offer praise to him for them.   We are not responsible for the results, only to give the cup. To give of ourselves. We must leave the results of our ministry in the hands of the master artist, God

How to interpret Art

God is everywhere, because he created everything, so anything that can be put on canvas displays something to be learned about his Kingdom. Therefore, artists who are not Christians still display the Character of God. Just as those who are not saved, have dreams related to God, so they can do art. Art is bringing to life a vision or dream. The bible is the primary way that God desires to speak to us. All who are born again to new life through a relationship with Jesus Christ to God as taking care of our sin will be able to hear from God.

The Bible says that , " As for you, the anointing which you received from Him abides in you, and you have no need for anyone to teach you; but as His anointing teaches you about all things, and is true and is not a lie, and just as it has taught you, you also will abide in the Son and in the Father (I John 2:24).

To interpret it according to God, you have e to follow his rules. Follow the steps in respect to the directory that he has laid out for us already. The Holy Bible.

1. **Ask God to help** you understand what he wants to teach you. He desires to teach us about his character, so he will always come through with this prayer.

2. **Look at the picture**. Take one item at a time. You may write down the words that depict the pictures. Often they have several meanings. Look them up in a dictionary. The message will be simple. It will also be multicultural. Generally, the message will be repeated several times throughout the painting.

3. **Look in the Bible** for the items. A concordance will help to find things.   The message of the should move us closer to God because that is the goal of God in all of His interactions with us.

For example: If there is a picture of a plow, search the scriptures and find verses with the word 'plow' in them. Then list the character of the plow. This leads you to what Gods wants to tell you. The message has something to do with being a 'sower of the word ' : one that prepares individuals to receive the seed of the Word (Jesus).

Another example: A picture of small trees growing in little pots on the stairs of the altar in a Church Sanctuary. If you research, you will see that God desires to make us to be a Church that plants seedlings. We are to be planted in good soil. (Isa 61:11). You might continue research and build on this foundation. More information is found about trees by following cross references in a regular Bible. Isa 61 has trees. Jesus also, talks about the seed being planted in Matt 13.

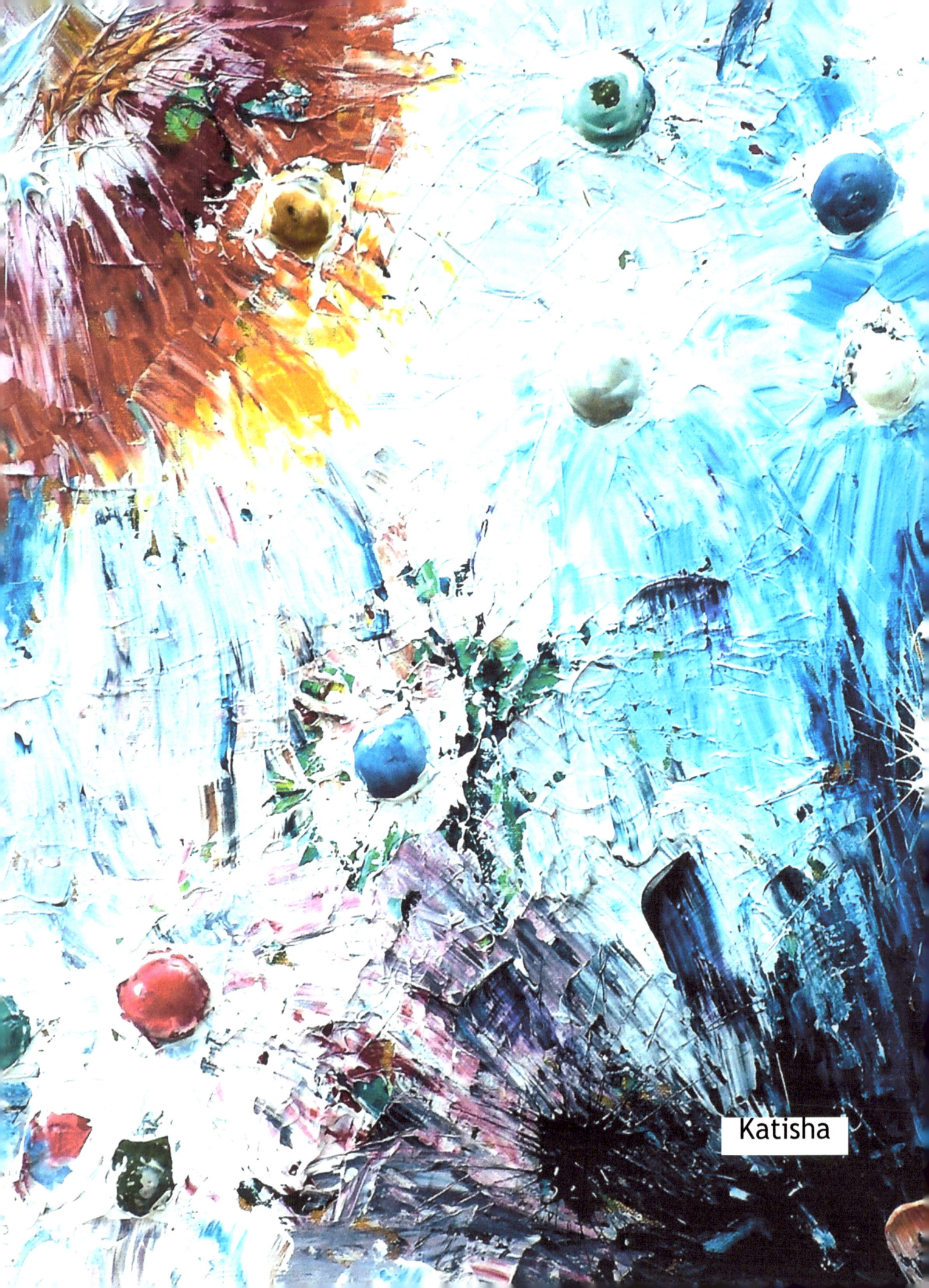

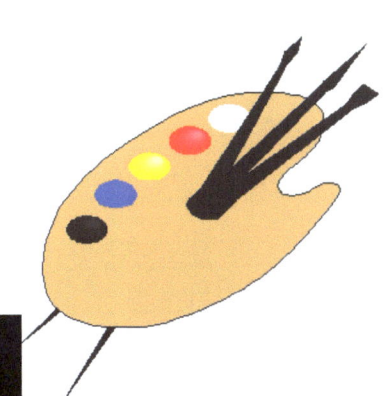

Index of Art:

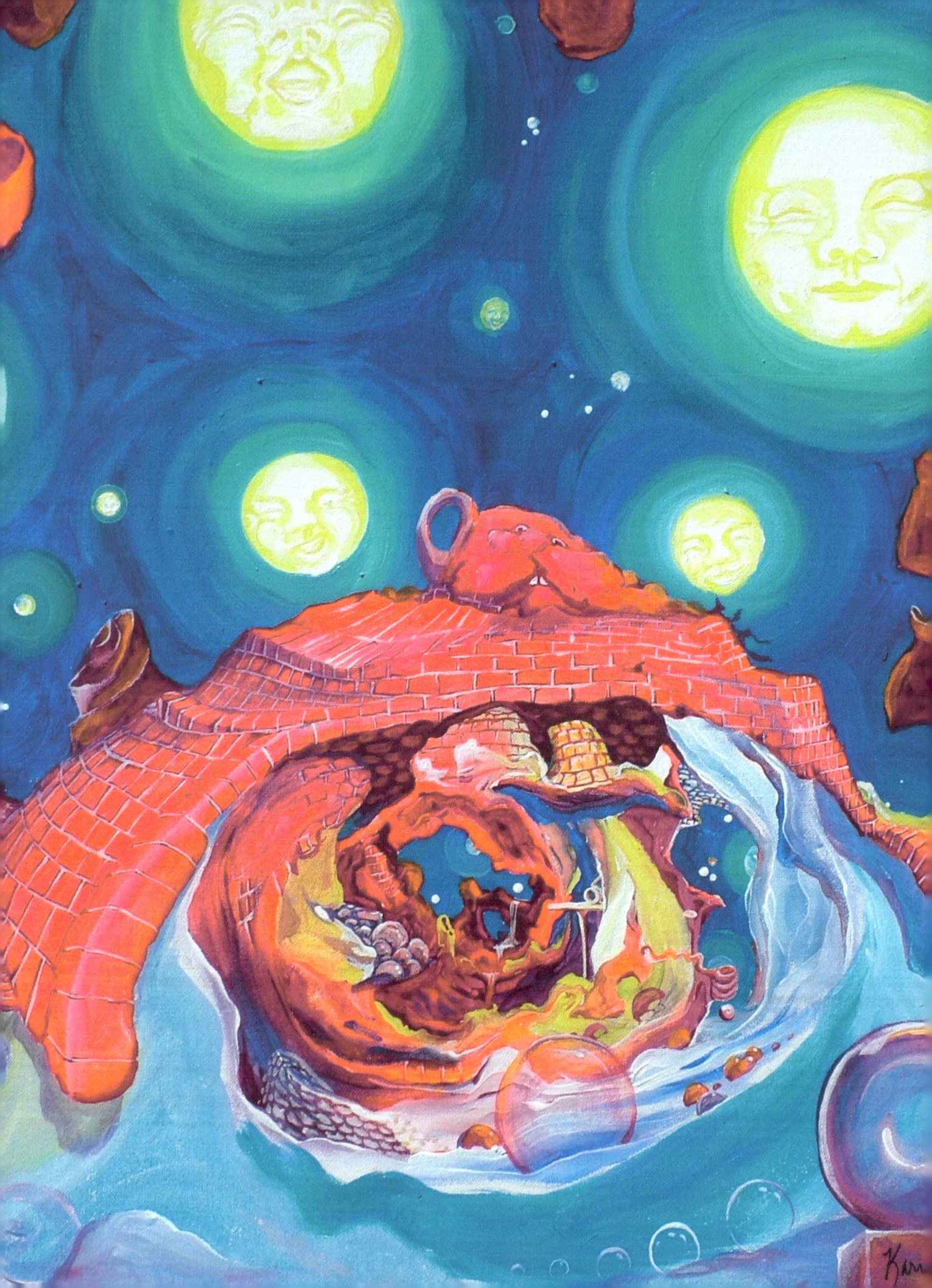

A Bump in the Road

As we follow the
red brick road, Satan
puts snares and trips along
the way. We must climb over whatever
we have buried in our own lives. There is
burring anger bound under this section of the
road.
There may be unresolved issues that have been
hidden. They are safe because they are hidden
deep within the snow. Jesus provides 'snow'
to cover our sins when we bring them to
him and ask forgiveness. The trash
in the air has also been brought
out to the light. Once it is
exposed to the
light
of the knowledge of God,
He will heal our lives.

The Rock

Purple
is the color
of royalty. God is King
of Kings, Lord of Lords and His works
are great among men. His power is endless
and to all eternity. God's arm is endowed with power
and strength. His right hand is exalted on high. He upholds
His word and is faithful to fulfill it. He has power over the depths
of the sea and the vast universe. All are moved by his word. Things
that
do not look possible are by the power of His word to us fulfilling
His promises. He will lead us to the rock that is higher than
us. It is a rock only to be stood on by faith. Our standing
does not depend on our desire or effort, but on
God's infinite mercy to us.
It is only through His loving kindness
that we stand on the rock -- and become like
little living rocks each having a place within the kingdom
of God -- all upheld by His right hand; the rock of His word.

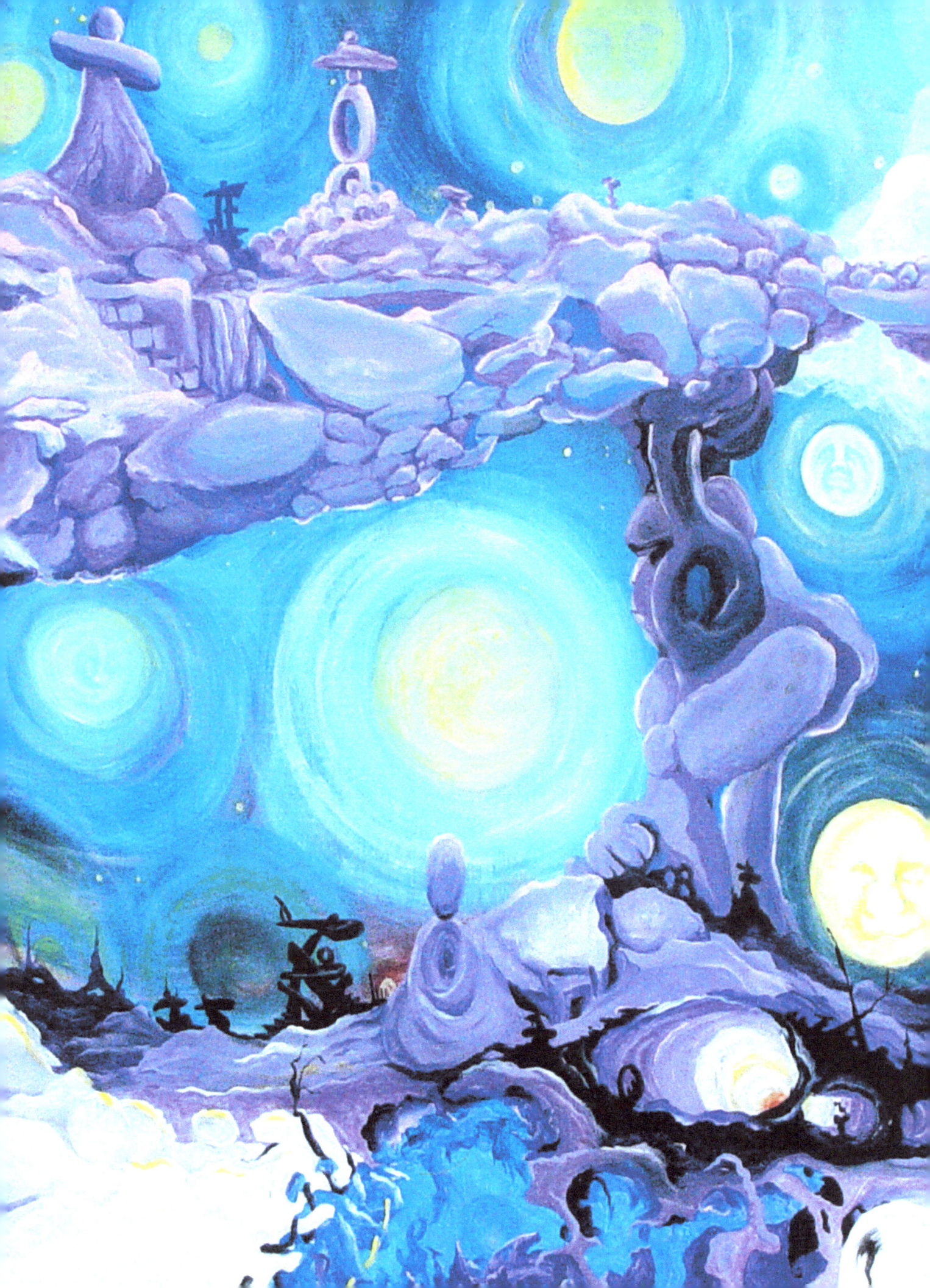

Buttons and Rope

Indeed the things which our Lord gives to us
are buttons and rope
fragrance and attachment.
And, does He give us buttons without any way to
sew them on?
Certainly not.
For God, Himself provides an attachment of the binding
of His precious love. When we become spiritually
attached to Heavenly things, then we
loose our attachment to the world.
This is a good thing.

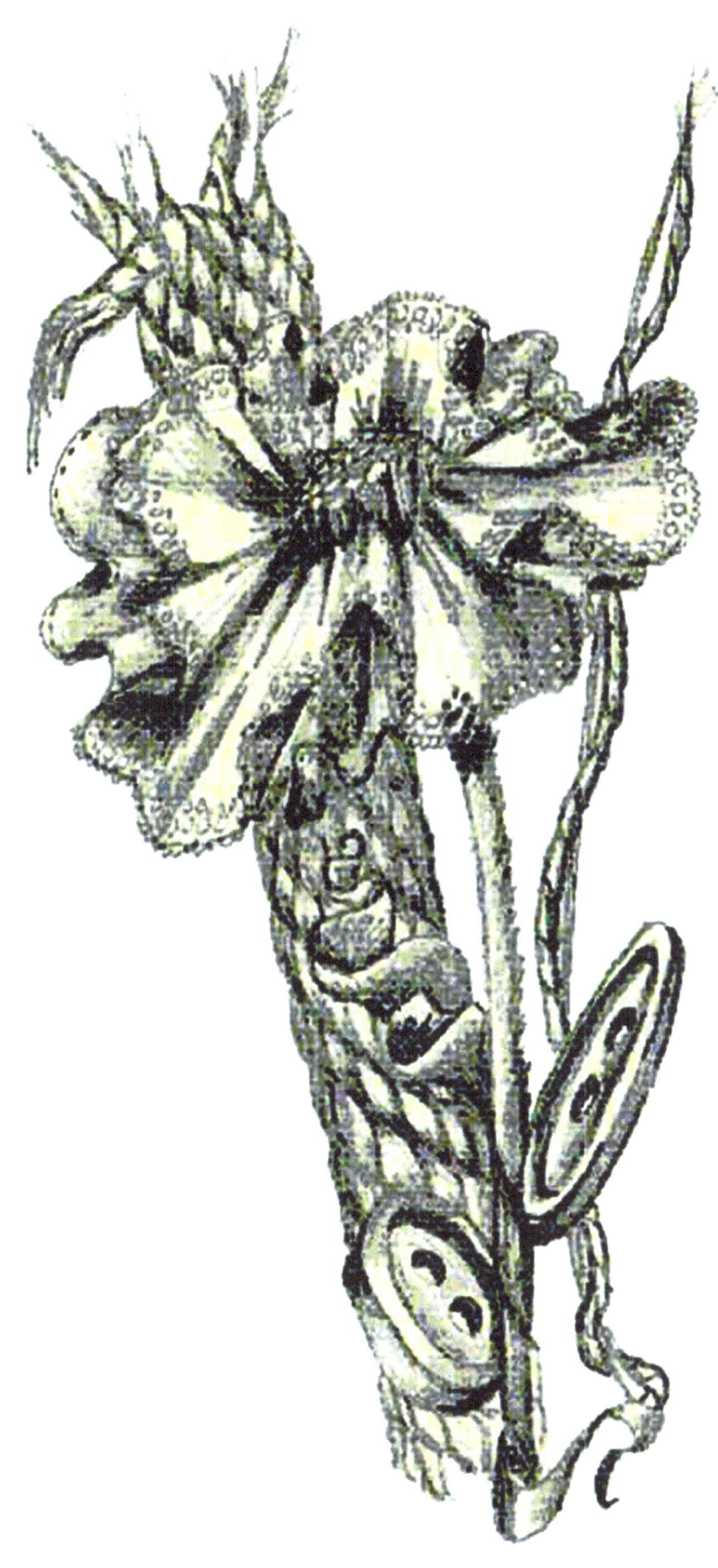

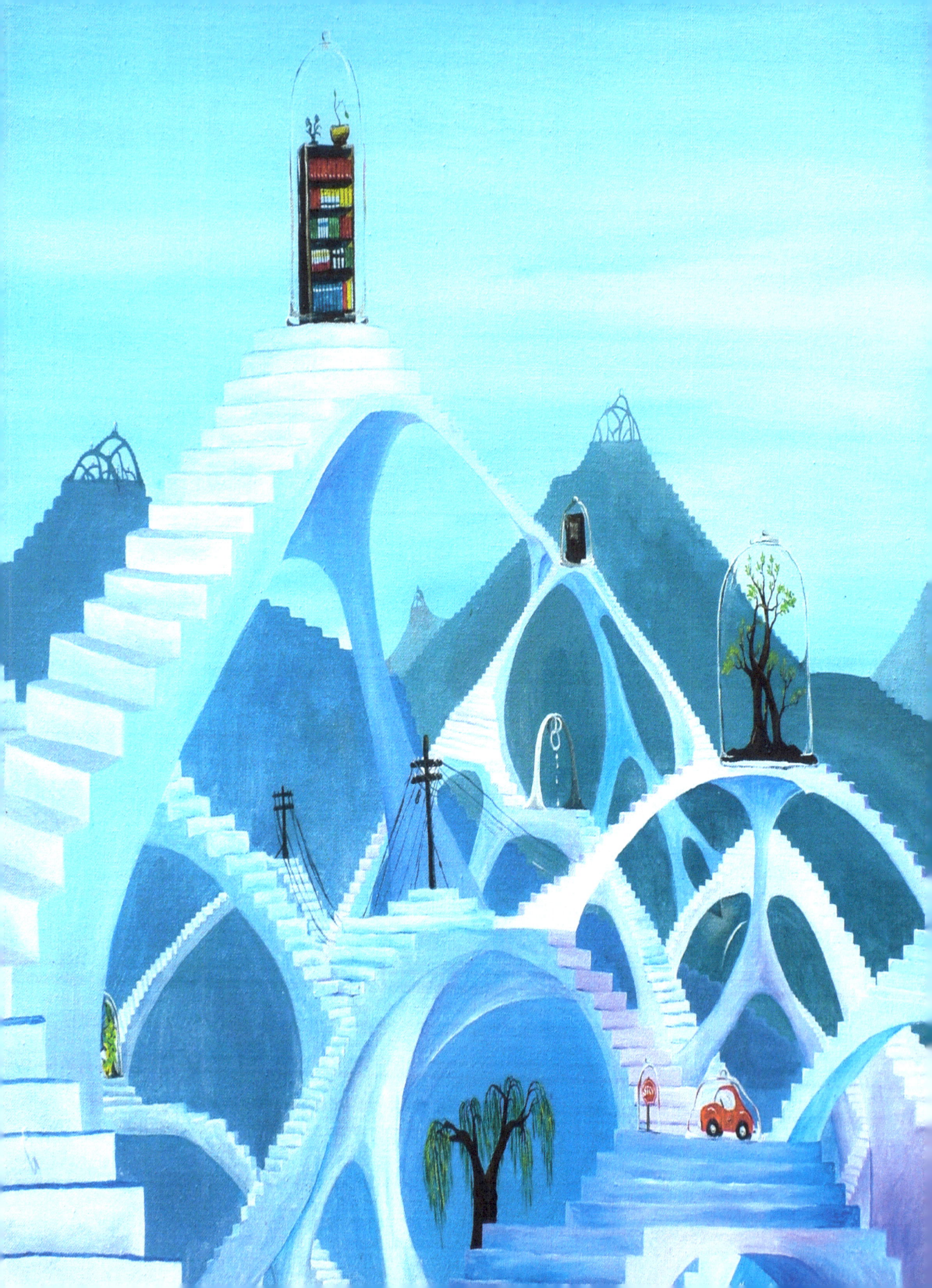

Stairway to Heaven

The steps to seeking God
lead upward and onward into eternity.
we move from one plane of glory to the next
as we move through the steps in our life. The bookcase
symbolizes knowledge. Though it will cost us all we have we
should acquire understanding of God. It is more precious than
Gold. The pathway to God is built around communication
with him along the way. The arch is a bow. It symbolizes a
covenant relationship that we must have with God to enter
into a right relationship with him. The three rings
are the Father, Son and the Holy Spirit.
As we pass under his care and
into his Kingdom,
he will rain righteousness
and blessings into our lives.
The tree is a symbol
of fruit that God
longs to produce
in our lives.
Fruit comes from
mature trees.
The leaves
are for
healing
of others
and our
fruit will provide
nourishment to others.
The vehicle shows us that we must
use what ever vehicle God has given us
for his Glory. Our talents must be given to him.
The door is Jesus Christ. We must open our hearts
to receive Him and walk through His forgiveness for our
sins. His door is ever open to us. He is close as we seeks Him
along our path ever upward onward on our steps from glory to glory.

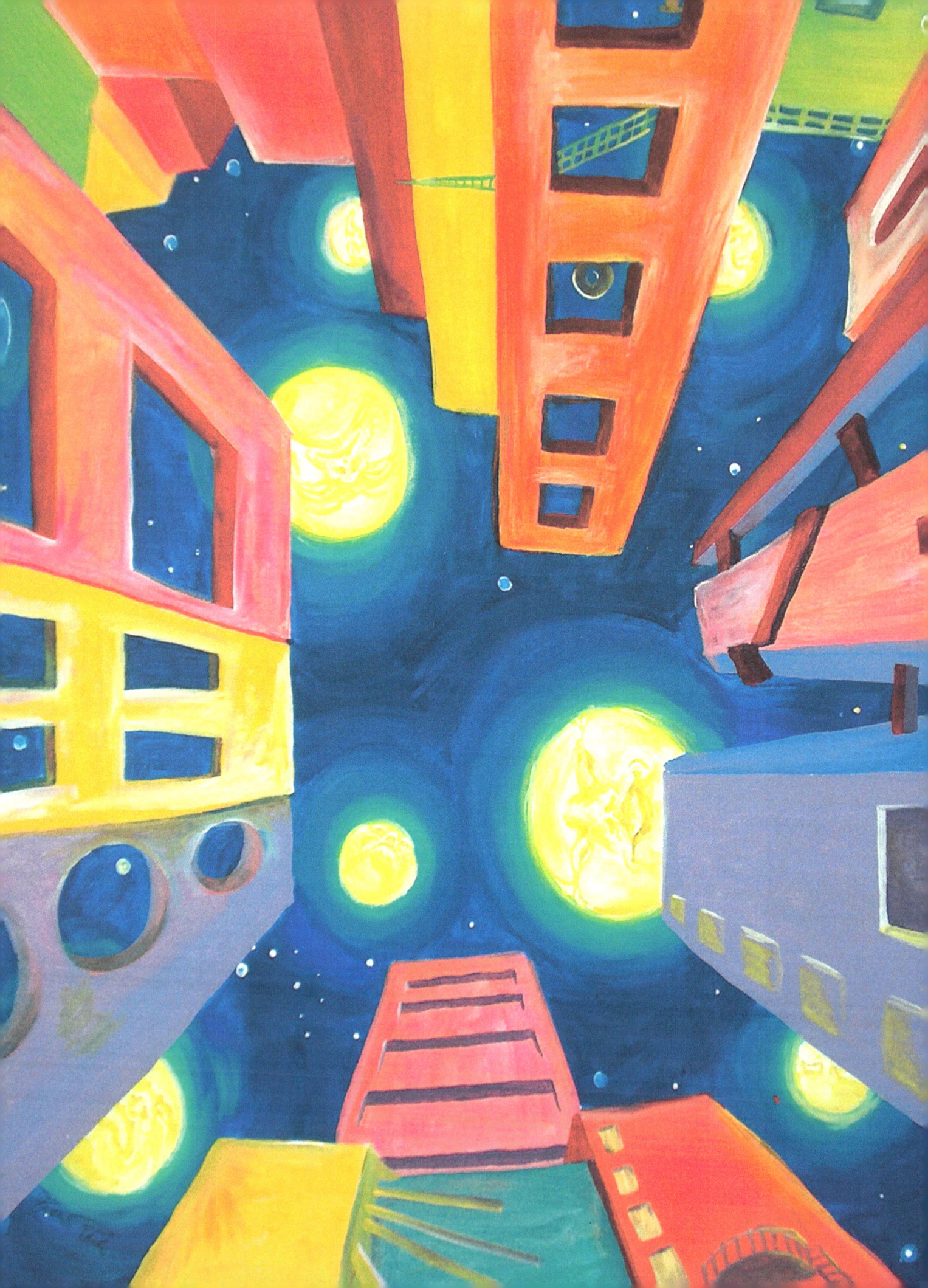

New Jerusalem: Eternal Glory

The angel who talked
with me had a measuring
rod of God to measure the city,
it's gates, and it's walls. The city was laid
out like a square... The walls was made of jasper, and
the city was of pure gold, pure as glass. The foundations of the
city walls were decorated with every precious stones. Jasper,
sapphire, chalcedony, emerald, sardonic, carnelian, chrysolite,
beryl,
topaz, chrysoprase, jacinth, amethyst. The twelve
gates were twelve pearls, each gate made of a
single pearl.
The great street of the city was
of pure gold, like transparent glass.
I did not see a temple in the city, because the
Lord God Almighty and the Lamb are its temple.
The city does not need the sun or the moon
to shine on it for the Glory of God
gives it light, and the Lamb
are its lamp.
The nations will walk
by its light, and the
kings of the earth
will
bring
their
splendor
into it.On
no day will its gates ever be shut,
for there will be no night there. Nothing
impure will ever enter it, nor will anyone who
does what is shameful or deceitful, but only those whose
names are written in the Lamb's book of life. Revelation 21:15-27.

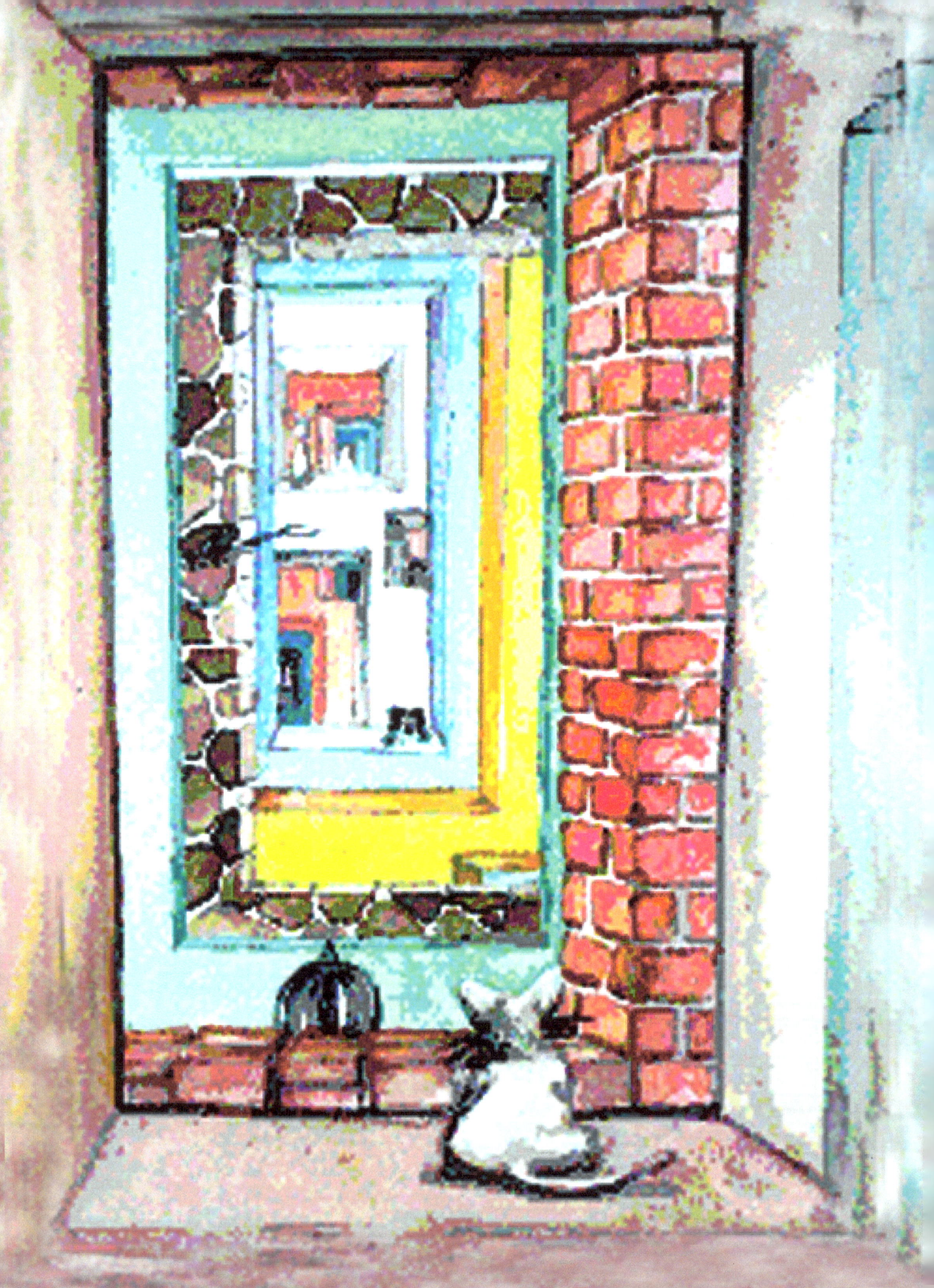

Open Doors

We have been given open doors and ope windows to see things beyond our world.

The walls of our understanding are as open as if the doors had been removed.

The Holy Spirit is the one who breaks through our understanding to allow us to see into other's lives {houses}.

And, they can see into us as well through the same peep hole of understanding called Prophecy.

Our Biography

A Few years ago when I began writing spiritual books, I visited Karna and Dean (her husband) for assistance with computer skills. I admit that they had a rough student because when I arrived I didn't even know how to cut and paste. I remember how amazed I was at the idea of putting page breaks into a book. Karna lives in Washington State nearby her grand-children and my brother, Roger. This picture was taken close to a house her and her husband built (with their two hands) which overlooks Maggy Lake. The house is just around the corner from my father. Karna has an extensive art gallery with paintings and murals hanging all over Belfair and Bremerton, Washington. I am proud to show off her art.

I worked full time as a heart nurse in Las Vegas for 30 years and then retired to commit to full-time publishing after moving to Camp Verde, Arizona. I am pretty busy with the company, dreaming and writing. My husband is a Commercial Pilot which gives me some time alone to get things done. I have two daughters, Stephanie and Esther who are married with five grandchildren. I have several books on prophecy. Picture on the left--Karna is wearing the fluffy coat and I have the plaid one on.   Sheri

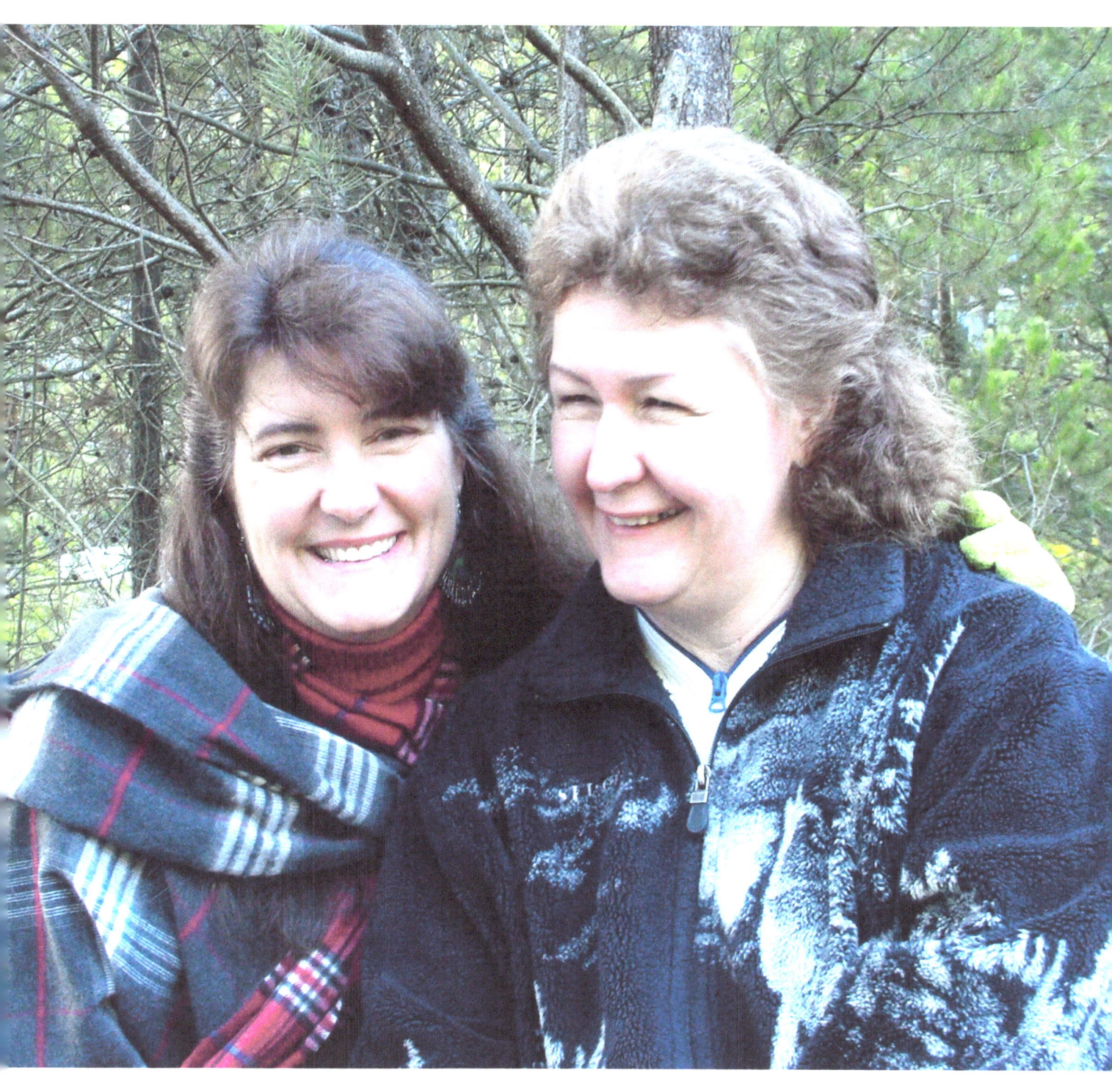

Author and Artist-- Sisters

Dream Cachë

Welcome to Sheri's dream cache releasing what has been kept hidden until now. There are
stores of riches kept in a vault up to this day, which open the door of understanding the
voice of God in dreams as answers to prayer. The wind, the storm, the rain and the
lightening of God is coming. Feel the wind? There is always a gentle breeze just
before the tornado. Oh how we have looked for the eye of the storm in this
world in which we live, yet we have not found it. We have prayed, yet we
are not healed. We have spent countless hours on our knees without
finding our deliverance. Our children remain on drugs; our families
are still in bondage; we are yet poor and destitute. Our Churches are
poor, filled with empty pews and singers off cue. Where are the answers
to our prayers? We have been tricked by our enemies. They have snuck in and
left seeds of doubt which grew into a cancer eating away at our faith in God. Our vision
has been clouded by our own
sinfulness and lust for the things of this world. Yet we continue to seek for a force outside
©ourselves which will save us from this dreadful condition which we are in. Where is He?
Take encouragement, friends, I have brought a fresh shipment of hope: It's the hope of
hearing the voice of God for yourself. Just like Moses heard the voice of the Lord and
brought Salvation to the Children of Israel, He is bringing the same today. Has God
changed? No. Suppose you ask a question in prayer: Do you expect an answer?
There is one, you know? I am here to help you reach out to God in a special way
and enable the enemies of doubt within your life to be crushed and conquered.
What I bring is a bridge to faith. We attempt to reach a God we do not
know; only have heard about from those going on before us. But, when
we reach into that darkness, we are unsure of a connection: Will there
be a hand reaching back to us? We don't really know. That is faith,
my friend. Faith reaches into the unknown seeking something you
are unsure of while trusting that there will be an answer on the
other side. Welcome to my dream Cachë. It is like a jewelry
box filled with gems, sparkling in the moonlight: dreams
that come to life as the voice of God dances through my
head night after night. And, He wants the same for
you. He told me, so. Your dreams and visions
can be a bridge to a relationship with God
giving encouragement, hope, help, and
direction hidden in this vault of
wondrous pictures
sent straight
from
heaven.
I have propped open
for you five doors
and a window .
I encourage
you to
learn to seek God through learning to understand His voice as it
comes to you His way, now as you are comfortable accepting it. Remember,
God came in thunder, storm and a wind in times before. Why wouldn't He now? May
I present this shipment of Grace. For it is by the Grace of God that we are saved. Remember that.

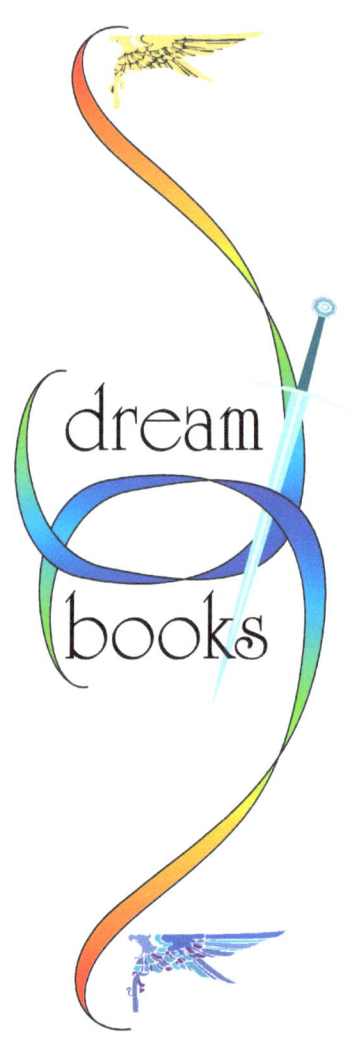